†

Letter
to a
Suffering
Church

A BISHOP SPEAKS ON THE
SEXUAL ABUSE CRISIS

BISHOP ROBERT BARRON

Word on Fire, Park Ridge, IL 60068
© 2019 by Word on Fire Catholic Ministries
Printed in the United States of America
All rights reserved.

22 21 20 19 2 3 4
ISBN: 978-1-943243-48-8

Library of Congress Control Number: 2019903919
Barron, Robert E.

www.wordonfire.org

TABLE OF
Contents

*T*his book is a *cri de cœur*, a cry from the heart. I am a lifelong Catholic, and I've been a priest for thirty-three years and a bishop for four years. I have dedicated my life to the Church. The sexual abuse scandal has been for me, for millions of other Catholics, and especially for the victim-survivors, lacerating. I have written this book for my fellow Catholics who feel, understandably, demoralized, scandalized, angry beyond words, and ready to quit. What I finally urge my brothers and sisters in the Church to do is to stay and fight—and to do so on behalf of themselves and their families, but especially on behalf of those who have suffered so grievously at the hands of wicked men. Of course, I'm also happy if those outside the Church find some illumination in these chapters as well.

I want to be clear about something at the outset: I am not speaking in the name of my brother bishops, or of the United States Conference of Catholic Bishops, or of the Vatican. I have no authority whatsoever to do so. I am speaking in my own name, as a Catholic, a priest, and a bishop. My prayer is that these reflections might encourage Catholics who are attempting to navigate today in very choppy waters.

CHAPTER ONE

The Devil's Masterpiece

*I*t has been a diabolical masterpiece. I am talking about the scandal that has gripped the Catholic Church for the past thirty years and that continues to wreak havoc even today. When I was going through the seminary, it was fashionable to conceive of the devil as a symbol for the evil in the world, a sort of colorful literary device. But the storm of wickedness that has compromised the work of the Church in every way and that has left countless lives in ruins is just too ingenious to have been the result of impersonal forces alone or merely human contrivance. It seems so thoroughly *thought through*, so comprehensively intentional. Certainly, in the ordinary run of history, bad things happen, but this scandal is just too exquisitely *designed*. It has corroded Catholic credibility so completely that the Church's work in evangelization, catechesis, preaching, outreach to the poor, recruitment of vocations, and education has been crippled. And most terribly, members of the Church, especially its most vulnerable, have been forced to live through a nightmare from which it seems impossible to wake. If the Church had a personal enemy—and indeed the devil is known as the enemy of the human race—it is hard to imagine that he could have come up with a better plan.

In saying this, I am by no means implying that human beings bear no responsibility; just the contrary. The devil works typically through suggestion, insinuation, temptation, and seduction. He is essentially powerless until he finds men and women who will cooperate with him. The best visual depiction of this dynamic is in a fresco by the early Renaissance painter Luca Signorelli, which can be found in the cathedral at Orvieto. It is a dramatic picture of the advent of the antichrist. The central figure, looking every inch the stereotypical Christ figure, is listening intently to the whispered suggestions of the devil, who presses in close to him. Only a careful examination reveals that what looks like the antichrist's left arm is in fact the arm of the devil, which has reached creepily through the antichrist's vesture. Whose voice is it? Whose gesture is it? Both the man's and the devil's. So it goes. And so it has gone these past several decades as the dark power, through far too many willing cooperators, has done his work.

Surveying the landscape of the Church today brings to mind a dismal and arresting passage from the book of the prophet Jeremiah. In the wake of the Babylonian devastation of the Israelite capital, the writer takes in the scene in and around Jerusalem: "If I go out to the country, Behold, those slain with the sword! Or if I enter the city, Behold, diseases of famine! For both prophet and priest have gone roving about in the land that they do not know" (Jer. 14:18). On the blasted and devastated ground today, landmarks have fallen, and even the insiders have lost their way. Conservative estimates indicate that the Catholic Church in the United States has

5

paid out four billion dollars in sex abuse settlements. Let that figure sink in. Four billion dollars that came, in large part, from the generous donations of Catholic people; four billion dollars that could have been used to build parishes, schools, universities, hospitals, and seminaries; four billion dollars that could have gone to educate children, to heal the sick, to care for the hungry and the homeless, to propagate the Gospel.

But that is an aspect of the devastation that is relatively easy to measure. The hurt and alienation felt by Catholics goes so far and deep that it is scarcely possible to gauge. Consider this: every particular act of sexual abuse by a priest establishes an extraordinary ripple effect through families, parishes, and communities. A single child might have been directly mistreated, but the anger, fear, and shame radiate out to mothers and fathers, aunts and uncles, brothers and sisters, friends and classmates. Now think of the thousands of cases of sexual abuse by clergy and the sickening influence that has gone out from each one of them. The rot has reached to virtually every cell and molecule in the Mystical Body of Christ.

That priests perpetrated this abuse makes it, of course, particularly awful. In accord with sound Catholic theology, the faithful have long taken priests to be not merely ministers or preachers but sacred figures, conformed in a unique way to Christ through ordination. The Spanish word for "priest" catches this nicely: *sacerdote* (holy one). Fr. Raniero Cantalamessa, preacher to the papal household, has said that, due to this unique identity, the smile of a priest is, for many Catholic people, the smile of God himself; a word of comfort from a priest is a word of comfort coming from the mouth of God. Tragically, this same logic obtains when priests become abusive. A child or teenager who was sexually assaulted by a priest felt violated by God, aggressed by the one he expected to be the source of greatest comfort and peace. The explosion that this cognitive dissonance has produced in the minds and souls of the abused is beyond staggering. It has given rise to a suffering that can only be characterized as metaphysical: the Creator of the world has turned into an enemy.

In the summer of 2018, the Attorney General of Pennsylvania issued a report of the cases of sexual abuse of minors by clergy in that state over roughly the previous seventy years. The number of abusive priests was depressing enough (roughly 300 priests and 1,000 victims), but the details of the cases sickened the Church—indeed, the whole country. A group of priests in the Pittsburgh diocese acted as a predatory ring, identifying potential candidates for abuse and passing information about them back and forth. They would take Polaroid photos of the children, in one case requesting a young man to take off his clothes and stand on the bed in the attitude of the crucified Jesus. To children that they found particularly attractive they would give gold crosses to wear around their necks, so as to signal their availability to other pedophile priests. One priest raped a young girl in the hospital, just after she had her tonsils removed. Another raped a girl, got her pregnant, and then arranged for the young woman to have an abortion. A Pittsburgh priest would give homeless boys drugs, money, and alcohol in exchange for sex. And while these crimes were being committed, the priests in question were typically removed from the parish or institution where the complaint originated but then reassigned somewhere else in the diocese, free to abuse again. As is now well established, this pattern of abuse, reassignment, and cover-up was repeated again and again across the Catholic world, fueling the massive frustration of the offended parties.

In that same terrible summer of 2018, it was revealed that then-Cardinal Theodore McCarrick, retired Archbishop of Washington, DC, had been a serial abuser throughout his clerical career. The case that broke open the story had to do with a young altar server whom McCarrick, then a priest of the Archdiocese of New York, sexually abused in the sacristy of St. Patrick's Cathedral just before Midnight Mass, as the boy was vesting for the liturgy. But as more and more victims came forward, it became clear that the Cardinal, in his various assignments as Bishop and Archbishop, preyed especially on seminarians, those young men over whom he had almost complete control. His favorite tactic was to invite those he found attractive to a beach house that he kept in New Jersey, always careful to include one more student than the beds in the place could accommodate, forcing one of them to sleep with him. One of his victims recounts a particularly sickening story of McCarrick watching the young man change into his bathing suit and subsequently, on the beach, slipping his hand under the seminarian's suit. If anyone wonders why these young men didn't object, run away, or punch the Cardinal in the face, he has to recall that these victims wanted—more than anything in the world—to be priests, and that McCarrick was the one who had the absolute power to determine whether that dream would be realized or not. And he was, as far as they were concerned, the supreme religious authority in their lives. To whom would they complain? The apostolic nuncio, the pope's American ambassador? Even supposing they knew such a person existed, they probably would have feared reaching out to him, presuming he either wouldn't believe them or would chastise them for bringing such a charge. In a word, it was a situation not unlike that involving young actors and actresses and their abusive studio bosses: the enormous power differential allowed the aggressor to get what he wanted and keep the victims quiet.

Just as bishop after bishop around the country quietly reshuffled abusive clergy from parish to parish, so it seems numerous bishops, archbishops, and cardinals, both in this country and in the Vatican, knew all about McCarrick's outrageous behavior and did nothing in response to it; or, rather worse, they continued to advance him up the ecclesiastical ladder, from auxiliary bishop, to bishop of a diocese, to archbishop, and finally to cardinal. Even after he resigned from his post in Washington, DC (immediately upon turning seventy-five, apparently at the urging of Pope Benedict XVI),

11

McCarrick continued to be a roving ambassador for the Church and a kingmaker in the American hierarchy—again, while everyone knew about his disturbing and abusive tendencies. The average Catholic in America could certainly be forgiven for thinking that something like a conspiracy of silence and a deep corruption obtain within the institutional life of the Church.

Just days before I composed these words, one of the most popular comedians in the United States, who happens to have been raised a Catholic, appeared on Saturday Night Live. In his monologue, he observed that his mother wondered whether his Jewish wife might one day convert to his Catholic faith. The audience immediately began giggling and guffawing in anticipation of his response. He gazed into the camera and said, "Can you imagine someone actually *voluntarily* choosing to become Catholic?" As the crowd broke into raucous laughter and applause, it struck me that things have gotten so bad that the comedian needed no further elaboration or explanation to get his laugh. It is just taken for granted that Catholicism is twisted and dysfunctional. I say this with deep regret, as a lifelong Catholic and as a bishop of the Church: Can we entirely blame them for making such an assumption?

In my capacity as Auxiliary Bishop of Los Angeles, I make frequent visits to the parishes in my pastoral region. In the wake of the McCarrick revelations and the Pennsylvania report, as I moved among the people of God, I came across anger, to be sure, but more frequently, tears. Standing in the vestibule of churches after Mass, dressed in the full liturgical regalia of a bishop, I functioned rather effectively as a symbol of Catholicism, and people would react to me and speak to me as such. In their bitter words and their even more bitter tears, I would sense both a deep love for the Church and a practically bottomless disillusionment with it. What was particularly galling about the McCarrick situation was that Catholics had heard, since 2002, that protocols and reforms were in place that would prevent abuse going forward. Now, real and substantive changes have indeed been put in place and they have made a significant difference (more on this later); nevertheless, I understood the frustration and the embarrassment. Many, many parishioners told me, after the McCarrick debacle, that they were once again ashamed to admit in public that they were Catholics. Just when they thought they were over the worst of the humiliation, the bottom fell out again. Again, I would emphasize that the frustration, anguish, and fury are grounded in a deep love for the Church and what it stands for. If people didn't fundamentally believe in the Church, they would not be so angry and so hurt over this disastrous and ongoing betrayal.

For years now, I've been tracing the phenomenon of the "nones"—that is to say, the religiously unaffiliated, those who have simply opted out of identification with a religious tradition. In the early 1970s, roughly 5% of Americans identified as having no religion. By the early 1990s, that figure had slightly risen to 6%, but it still indicated a relatively small number of people. But today, the percentage of religiously unaffiliated in our country is 25%! One quarter of Americans now claim no religion at all. The count is even more striking when we narrow our focus to the young. The percentage of "nones" under the age of thirty rises to 40%, and among Catholic youth, the figure is an incredible 50%. Also, studies have indicated that for every one person who joins the Catholic Church today, roughly six are abandoning their Catholicism. There are, of course, multiple causes for this dramatic increase in disaffiliation, especially among Catholics, but all the surveys clearly state, to no one's great surprise, that the clergy scandals have contributed significantly to a loss of confidence in the Church. I am just as concerned about these armies of young people who are simply walking away from the Church as I am about those who, crying tears of rage, hang on. In regard to the latter group, I can appeal to the affection that still remains. But in regard to the former, it is much more difficult to get any traction.

So, many Catholics are understandably asking, "Why should I stay? Why not abandon this sinking ship before it drags me or my children under?" It is my conviction that this is not the time to leave; it is the time to stay and fight. The Scriptures shed a great deal of light on our present situation; we've been here before in our history and we've survived; everything you love in the Church is still present and is worth defending; there is a path forward. If you're willing to read on, I will try in brief compass to defend each of these claims.

Has this explosion of wickedness been the devil's masterpiece? Yes. But Jesus said that the gates of hell would not prevail against his Church. Do the powers of darkness seem triumphant? Perhaps. But the Lord promised us he would never leave us, even until the end of the age. So we are forbidden to give up hope.

CHAPTER TWO

Light from Scripture

*T*his terrible crisis has, God knows, been analyzed from numerous perspectives: psychological, interpersonal, criminal, cultural, etc. These are all valid and illuminating paths, but the problem will not be adequately investigated until it is seen in the light that comes from the Word of God. And it turns out that the Bible has a great deal to say about human sexuality, both what it is supposed to be in the plan of God and the myriad ways that sin twists and distorts it. The Bible is not the least opposed to bodiliness or sex. In fact, over and against all forms of dualism, it insists that everything that God has made— from the stars and planets to animals and insects—is good. Moreover, practically the first command that God gives to human beings in the Garden of Eden is to be fruitful and multiply. And whenever

God makes a covenant with his chosen people, he seals it, as it were, with the injunction that they go forth and have many children. Throughout the Scriptures, marriage is used as a master metaphor for the passionate, faithful, and life-giving love that God has for his people Israel. In a word, sex is not a problem; it is, instead, a kind of sacrament.

On the biblical reading, trouble arises when sex is wrenched out of the context of love and used as a tool of domination or manipulation. In accord with the ancient adage *corruptio optimi pessima* (the corruption of the best is the worst), distorted sexuality becomes a vivid countersign of the divine. The sacred authors offer a number of examples of what this reversal looks like.

I should first like to consider the strange but richly illuminating story from the eighteenth and nineteenth chapters of the book of Genesis, which treats of an angelic visit to the patriarch Abraham and its troubling aftermath. We are told that the Lord appeared to Abraham through the mediation of three angelic figures. After the patriarch received and served them, the visitors predicted that, despite their advanced years, Abraham and Sarah would have a son a year hence. Overhearing the conversation, Sarah laughs at the absurdity of the suggestion that she and her husband could still experience "sexual pleasure," but the Lord remonstrated with Abraham, "Why did Sarah laugh and say, 'Will I really bear a child, old as I am?' Is anything too marvelous for the Lord to do?" (Gen. 18:13-14). What is marvelous, of course, is not simply that an elderly woman would bear a son, but that the promise made to Abraham—that he would become the father of a great nation—was, against all odds, about to come true. God's lordship, faithful human cooperation, the fulfillment of the covenant, reproduction, laughter, and even sexual pleasure are all, in the typically Israelite manner, folded in together.

And this is why it is extremely instructive to examine the stories of sexual perversion and misconduct that immediately follow this one, for they demonstrate the negation of God's plan for human sexuality. At the beginning of the nineteenth chapter of Genesis, we hear that the angels who had visited Abraham have made their way to the city of Sodom, the home of Abraham's nephew Lot. After enjoying a meal in Lot's home, the angels find themselves hemmed in by a startlingly aggressive and lustful band of men—indeed, we are told, *all* of the men, both young and old, of the town. Without the slightest hesitation or shame, they announce their intentions: "Where are the men who came to your house tonight? Bring them out to us that we may have intimacies with them" (Gen. 19:5). The gang rape being proposed—violent, impersonal, self-interested, and infertile—is the precise opposite of what God intends for human sexuality. In the feral men of Sodom, the image of God has been almost completely obscured.

The narrative becomes, if anything, more unnerving as we consider the reaction of Lot. The nephew of Abraham begins promisingly enough: "I beg you, my brothers, not to do this wicked thing." But then he proposes a rather appalling solution: "I have two daughters who have never had intercourse with men. Let me bring them out to you, and you may do to them as you please" (Gen. 19:7-8). In order to stave off a brutal sexual assault, he presents his own virgin daughters for a violent gang rape. Could we imagine a more thoroughgoing undermining of the Creator's intention regarding sex? The men of Sodom, simmering with rage, are having none of it, and they press Lot against the door of his home. At this point, the angels intervene, pulling Lot inside and striking the men of the mob blind. The dramatic intervention should not be read simply as an intriguing twist in the narrative, but rather as the symbolic communication of a spiritual dynamic. Having devolved morally to the level of pack animals, the men of Sodom have become blind to any of the deeper dimensions of sexuality and human community. In response to the polymorphous dysfunction of the city, God, we are told, rained fire and brimstone upon Sodom. We must never interpret divine punishment in the Bible as arbitrary or the result of an emotional affront; rather, we should read it as a sort of spiritual physics, God allowing the natural consequences of sin to obtain.

Following the destruction of Sodom and Gomorrah, Lot and his daughters, we are told, flee to the surrounding hill country, where they take up residence in a cave. Musing on the annihilation of their city, Lot's older daughter suggests to the younger that since all the men have been wiped out, they should couple with their father and so bring forth children. Accordingly, on successive nights, they get their father drunk and sleep with him, and through these incestuous relations, both girls become pregnant. They thereby give rise to the Moabites and the Ammonites, two tribes that, in time, would come to be at odds with Israel. Can anyone miss the connection between the shocking psychological and sexual abuse to which these girls were subjected—their own father offering them to a violent mob—and their subsequent abuse of Lot? Haven't we seen over and again in our time the sadly familiar dynamic of sexual abuse begetting sexual abuse, the sin passed on like a contagion from generation to generation? That this perversion of sexuality took place in a cave, the dwelling place of animals and primitives, is still another indication that the *imago Dei* has been rather thoroughly effaced. And that the warped unions are the source of two peoples antagonistic to Israel is a further sign that what transpired between Lot and his daughters stands completely athwart God's purpose.

The narrative of Eli and his sons, recounted in the first book of Samuel, is an eerily accurate anticipation of many of the features of the clergy sex abuse scandal of the present day. The first glimpse we get of Eli, high priest of Shiloh, is not edifying. Demonstrating not an ounce of pastoral sensitivity, Eli upbraids the distraught Hannah, who had been praying aloud in the sacred place, begging God for a child: "How long will you make a drunken show of yourself? Sober up from your wine!" (1 Sam. 1:14). Then we hear of Eli's sons, Hophni and Phineas, who are priests like their father, but wicked, having regard neither for God nor for the people. We are told that they took the best meat from the sacrifices piously offered by the supplicants at Shiloh and that they were sexually abusing the women who worked at the entry of the meeting tent. The victims of their abuse brought complaints to Eli, and the high priest responded with strong enough words, remonstrating with his sons, "No, my sons, you must not do these things! It is not a good report that I hear the people of the Lord spreading about you. If a man sins against another man, one can intercede for him with the Lord; but if a man sins against the Lord, who can intercede for him?" (1 Sam. 2:24-25). But Hophni and Phineas disregarded their father's warning and continued on their path of corruption, and Eli apparently took no further action against his sons.

It is against this background that we must read the famous and poignant story of the Lord's call to Samuel, the son whom Hannah had sought from the Lord and whom she had given to the Lord for service in the temple. We are told that, at this time, "a revelation of the Lord was uncommon and vision infrequent" (1 Sam. 3:1). One might be permitted to wonder whether this was a function of the Lord's refusal to speak or rather of the blindness and corruption of the spiritual leadership of the nation. During the night, God calls to Samuel, but neither the boy nor his spiritual father understand the nature of the summons. Only after several false starts does Eli give the proper instruction: "If you are called, reply, 'Speak, Lord, for your servant is listening'" (1 Sam. 3:9). Since the version of this narrative that is found in the lectionary ends at this point, most Catholics don't know the devastating words that the Lord finally speaks to young Samuel: "I am about to do something in Israel that will cause the ears of everyone who hears it to ring. On that day I will carry out in full against Eli everything I threatened against his family" (1 Sam. 3:11-12). And God specifies precisely why he will exact such a severe punishment: "I announce to him that I am condemning his family once and for all, because of this crime: though he knew his sons were blaspheming God, he did not reprove them" (1 Sam. 3:13). In short, it was not the crimes of Hophni and Phineas that particularly aroused the divine ire, but rather Eli's refusal to act when he was made aware of them.

Just after this unnerving revelation, the Philistines engaged Israel in battle, and the result was an unmitigated disaster. After four thousand Israelites were slain in a preliminary skirmish, the army regrouped and resolved to bring the Ark of the Covenant itself into battle. Despite the presence of this talisman of the God who had brought Israel out of Egypt, the Philistines won a decisive victory, killing thirty thousand Israelites, including Hophni and Phineas, and carrying away the Ark as booty. When news of the catastrophe reached Eli, the old priest was sitting by the gate of Shiloh. So overwhelmed was he that he fell over backward and broke his neck, thus bringing—as the Lord had predicted—his entire family to an end.

Now, does any of this story strike you as familiar? We hear of priests abusing their people both financially and sexually; complaints are brought to their superior, who uses strong words and promises decisive action but does nothing to stop the abuse. And the result of this double failure is a disaster and deep shame for the entire people, as they are delivered into the hands of their enemies. I would suggest that the story of Eli and his sons is an almost perfect biblical icon of the sexual abuse scandal that has unfolded over the past thirty years. At the apparent height of the troubles, in the early 2000s, many Catholics in America were dismayed at the frank anti-Catholicism on display in many of the newspapers, journals, and television stations that covered the scandal. Those with a biblical frame of reference shouldn't have been surprised: the new Israel of the Church had been handed over to its enemies, precisely for the sake of purification.

The endlessly fascinating and psychologically complex tale of David and Bathsheba, recounted in the eleventh and twelfth chapters of 2 Samuel, has beguiled artists, poets, and spiritual writers across the centuries. It is one of the most sensitive and subtle narratives that has come down to us from the ancient world, and it sheds a good deal of light on our subject.

The commencement of the story is worth close attention: "At the turn of the year, when kings go out on campaign," David "remained in Jerusalem" (2 Sam. 11:1). David was the greatest of Israel's campaigners, never shrinking from a fight, always at the head of the army, willing to undertake even the most dangerous missions. So why is he lingering at home, precisely at the time of year when kings typically sally forth? A clue to David's reticence is provided in the next verse: "One evening David rose from his siesta and strolled about on the roof of the palace" (2 Sam. 11:2). To be sure, people in Mediterranean cultures typically take a siesta after the midday meal, but it is significant that the king rose *in the evening*, implying that he had been in bed quite some time. What the biblical author sketches here, in characteristically laconic manner, is a portrait of a king gone to seed, a military leader grown a bit indulgent and indifferent. When he was in his spiritual prime, David invariably inquired of God what he should do, even in regard to minor matters; but throughout the Bathsheba narrative, he never asks God for direction. Rather, he does the directing. From his godlike vantage point on the rooftop of his palace, David can see in every direction, and he can order things according to his whim. It is precisely from this perspective that he spies the beautiful Bathsheba, wife of Uriah the Hittite, and through a series of quick and staccato commands, takes her to himself. The biblical author is likely aware of Bathsheba's own cooperation with the affair—does she just happen to be bathing within easy eyeshot of the king?—but he is especially interested in the king's deft but wicked use of his power to manipulate another.

In the wake of Bathsheba's pregnancy, David attempts to cover up his sin using every means at his disposal, cruelly playing with the upright Uriah who, though an outsider, nevertheless proves more faithful to Israel's laws than does Israel's king. Finally, of course, David arranges things so as to bring about Uriah's death, stooping so low as to compel the man himself to unwittingly carry his own order of execution to Joab, the commander in the field. The murder of Uriah allowed David to take Bathsheba as his wife and definitively to cover up his sin, but we are told that "the Lord was displeased with what David had done" (2 Sam. 11:27). Again and again, the Scriptures insist that any human power is grounded in and derived from a more fundamental divine sovereignty. No matter how much rangy authority a human being has, he does not escape the moral oversight and sanction of God. This is the sense of Jesus' reminder to Pilate, the representative of the most powerful political institution of his time: "You would have no power over me if it had not been given to you from above"

(John 19:11). In his laziness, self-indulgence, manipulation, and cruelty, David stands here as an icon of the abuse of power.

After this brief tour of some Old Testament narratives, I would like to conclude this biblical section with a look at Jesus in relation to children. The eighteenth chapter of Matthew's Gospel commences with a lovely and incisive meditation on the spiritual significance of children and of Jesus' attitude toward them. Exhibiting their customary tendency to miss the point, Jesus' entire company of disciples approached him with the question, "Who is the greatest in the kingdom of heaven?" (Matt. 18:1). Their inquiry, of course, is born of a false or fallen consciousness, a preoccupation with honor and worldly power. In answer, Jesus called a little child over and placed him in their midst—which is to say, in the focal point, the center. By so situating the child, he physically interrupted their jockeying for position and notice. In his innocence and humility, the child exemplifies what the spiritual masters call the true self, which is able to relate simply and directly to reality. This is in opposition to the false self, which is so layered over with preoccupations with honor that it gets at reality only haltingly and through a kind of buffer. Though they take on the qualities of the false self soon enough, little children typically exemplify this spiritual alertness precisely in their ability to lose themselves in a game or a conversation or the beautiful facticity of the simplest things.

It was a commonplace in the ancient world to hold up distinguished figures as models: military commanders, religious leaders, political potentates, etc. But what Jesus is doing is turning this tradition on its head, placing in the position of honor a figure of no social prominence, no influence, no connections. Within the standard societal framework of the time, children were expected to remain silent, and it was assumed that the powerful could manipulate them at will. Jesus reverses this, identifying the socially negligible as the greatest. Indeed, for those who have moved from the false self to the true self, the very meaning of greatness has been adjusted: "Whoever humbles himself like this child is the greatest in the kingdom of heaven" (Matt. 18:4).

What follows is a remark of rich theological significance: "And whoever receives one child such as this in my name receives me" (Matt. 18:5). In the second chapter of Philippians, we find the exquisite hymn that Paul has adapted to his purposes. It commences with an evocation of the self-emptying quality of the Son of God who, "though he was in the form of God, did not regard equality with God something to be grasped. Rather, he emptied himself, taking the form of a slave, coming in human likeness; and found human in appearance, he humbled himself, becoming obedient to death, even death on a cross" (Phil. 2:6-8). In short, the child—humble, simple, self-effacing—functions as a sort of iconic representation of the divine Child of the divine Father. The route of access to Jesus is therefore to move into the spiritual space of a child, to "accept" him in the fullest sense. This truth becomes especially clear in Mark's version of this story. When the disciples disputed about which of them is greatest, Jesus said, "If anyone wishes to be first, he shall be the last of all and the servant of all" (Mark 9:35). Then he took a child and, in a gesture of irresistible poignancy, placed his arms around him, simultaneously embracing, protecting, and offering him as an example. The clear implication is that the failure to accept, protect, and love a child—or, what is worse, the active harming of a child—would preclude real contact with Jesus.

And this helps to explain the vehemence of the statement that immediately follows: "Whoever causes one of these little ones who believe in me to sin, it would be better for him to have a great millstone hung around his neck and to be drowned in the depths of the sea" (Matt. 18:6). Mind you, this is from the mouth of the same Jesus who, just a few chapters before, had urged the love of enemies! I don't think for a moment that the earlier teaching is being repudiated, but I do indeed think that the extraordinary gravity of the offense is being emphasized. There is no other sin—not hypocrisy, not adultery, not indifference to the poor—that Jesus condemns with greater passion than this: "Woe to the world because of things that cause sin! Such things must come, but woe to the one through whom they come. If your hand or foot causes you to sin, cut it off and throw it away. It is better for you to enter life maimed or crippled than with two hands or two feet to be thrown into eternal fire. And if your eye causes you to sin, tear it out and throw it away. It is better for you to enter into life with one eye than with two eyes to be thrown into fiery Gehenna" (Matt. 18:7-9). It cannot possibly be accidental that Jesus mentions Gehenna in the context of condemning those who attack children, for Gehenna was the place where, throughout much of the Old Testament period, children were sacrificed to idols.

This extraordinary section concludes with an evocation of the angels: "See that you do not despise one of these little ones, for I say to you that their angels in heaven always look upon the face of my heavenly Father" (Matt. 18:10). This is far more than pious decoration. The abuse of children is a function of the objectification of children, turning them, as we saw, into mere means. In reminding his listeners that every child is assigned a supernatural guide who is, in turn, intimately linked to God, Jesus is insisting upon the incomparable dignity of those whom society—then and now—is likely to disregard or undervalue. The central tragedy of the sexual abuse scandal is that those who were ordained to act in the very person of Christ became, in the most dramatic way, obstacles to Christ.

CHAPTER THREE

We Have Been Here Before

*T*here is, to be sure, a unique texture to the crisis we are presently enduring. Precisely because it involves, on such a massive scale, the abuse of young people by men meant by ordination to be distinctively configured to Christ, it is peculiarly twisted and sickening. I would furthermore contend that it certainly constitutes the darkest moment in the history of the Church in the United States, far surpassing the aggressive persecution of Catholics that took place in the nineteenth century. At the same time, I want to insist that the current darkness must be seen in historical perspective. The Church, from the very beginning and at every point in its development, has been marked to varying degrees by sin, scandal, stupidity, misbehavior, misfortune, and wickedness. Commenting upon dysfunction within the very first Christian communities, St. Paul said something that has shed light up and down the ages: "We hold this treasure in earthen vessels" (2 Cor. 4:7). The treasure is the grace of Christ, the new life made available through the dying and rising of Jesus, and the vessels are the deeply flawed, fragile, and morally suspect people who have received that grace and who are endeavoring to live that new life.

Eighteen hundred years after Paul, John Henry Newman, one of the most perceptive theological minds in the tradition, made this rather startling and sweeping observation: "The whole course of Christianity . . . is but one series of troubles and disorders. Every century is like every other, and to those who live in it seems worse than all times before it. The Church is ever ailing . . . Religion seems ever expiring, schisms dominant, the light of truth dim, its adherents scattered. The cause of Christ is ever in its last agony."

And lest we think that the corruption of priests and bishops is unique to our time, we should recall one of the wittiest rejoinders in Church history. The Emperor Napoleon is said to have confronted Cardinal Consalvi, the secretary of state to Pope Pius VII, saying that he, Napoleon, would destroy the Church—to which the Cardinal deftly responded, "Oh my little man, you think you're going to succeed in accomplishing what centuries of priests and bishops have tried and failed to do?" In a similar vein, the early twentieth-century Catholic writer Hilaire Belloc made this rather acid observation in reference to the moral and intellectual quality of the Church's leadership: "The Catholic Church is an institution I am bound to hold divine—but for unbelievers a proof of its divinity might be found in the fact that no merely human institution conducted with such knavish imbecility would have lasted a fortnight."

When I was a first-year seminarian, I took a course in Church history taught by a legendary Chicago priest, Msgr. Charles Meyer. Naturally, Msgr. Meyer rehearsed the key events, the pivotal dates, and the heroic players across the two millennia of the Church's life, but he took a particular, even slightly devilish, delight in recounting the numerous misdeeds and outrageous sins of priests, bishops, and popes. I will admit that many of us were initially scandalized by this litany of crimes, but I came eventually to see Msgr. Meyer's course as a real, though odd, grace. Hearing these dark tales was a bit like receiving an immunization. Having taken in the very worst of Church history, we could even more clearly understand that there is nevertheless something good, even indestructibly good, about the Mystical Body of Christ. And therefore, we were less likely to despair of the project. It is with this "immunizing" purpose that I write this chapter.

There is, in the Acts of the Apostles, an idyllic account of life in the primitive Church. The first followers of Jesus, we are told, engaged in prayer and service of the poor, and each member of the community placed his goods at the feet of the Apostles for the benefit of the most needy. But trouble set in soon enough. In his first letter to the tiny Christian family that he had established in Corinth, St. Paul upbraided the Church for the factionalism and divisions that had already arisen: "For it has been reported to me about you, my brothers, by Chloe's people, that there are rivalries among you. . . . Is Christ divided?" (1 Cor. 1:11, 13). We find much the same thing in his letter to the Romans: "I urge you, brothers, to watch out for those who create dissensions and obstacles, in opposition to the teaching that you learned" (Rom. 16:17). We also hear, in these earliest Christian texts, of sexual misconduct in the Church. Listen again to Paul in first Corinthians: "It is widely reported that there is immorality among you, and immorality of a kind not found even among pagans—a man living with his father's wife" (1 Cor. 5:1). And a bit later in the same letter, we hear: "Do you not know that your bodies are members of Christ? Shall I then take Christ's members and make them the members of a prostitute? Of course not!" (1 Cor. 6:15). And we find this rather remarkable summary statement in the letter to the Galatians: "Now the works of the flesh are obvious: immorality, impurity, licentiousness, idolatry, sorcery, hatreds, rivalry, jealousy . . . occasions of envy, drinking bouts, orgies, and the like. I warn you . . . that those who do such things will not inherit the kingdom of God" (Gal. 5:19-21). It goes without saying, of course, that Paul wouldn't have delineated these misbehaviors were they not actually present in the community.

If we move forward a few centuries from the time of Paul, we come to the dawn of the monastic movement within Christianity. Figures such as Antony of the Desert in the East and Benedict of Nursia in the West sought refuge from a world that they perceived as hopelessly corrupt—and mind you, the "world" in question was, at least in principle, Christian. The young Benedict, for example, was so scandalized by the immorality on display in Rome where he had come to study that he fled to a cave in Subiaco. In the isolation of that place, he commenced to live as a hermit, and the first monks of the Benedictine movement were those who were drawn by his austere example.

The office of Peter has been filled by a number of saintly and accomplished men over the ages, but it has also been occupied by far more questionable figures. The tenth and eleventh centuries were particularly characterized by papal corruption. Arguably the worst pontiff in history was John XII, who reigned from 955 to 964. John's wickedness was so egregious that bishops and cardinals endeavored to remove him. Gathered in synod, they accused him of "sacrilege, simony, perjury, murder, adultery, and incest." Summoned to defend himself against these charges, John instead excommunicated his accusers and executed judgment on them, striking off the hand of one, scourging another, and removing the nose and ears of a third. Pope John died in the act of coitus, either from apoplexy or by the murderous hand of an offended rival.

John had some competition for the title of worst pope in history from a successor in the eleventh century—namely, Benedict IX. This man became pope when he was a layman in his early twenties, the beneficiary of family influence and intrigue. While occupying the throne of Peter, his lifestyle was "straight out of Suetonius . . . marked by allegations of rape, murder, bribery, adultery, and sodomy." Here is how one nineteenth-century historian summed up Benedict's character: "It seemed as if a demon from hell, in the disguise of a priest, occupied the chair of Peter and profaned the sacred mysteries of religion by his insolent courses." One of his successors, Pope Victor III, referred to "his rapes, murders, and other unspeakable acts of violence and sodomy," and he concluded, "his life as a pope was so vile, so foul, so execrable that I shudder to think of it."

As we consider the corruption of Church leaders, three literary figures come readily to mind: one from the fourteenth century, one from the fifteenth, and one from the sixteenth. I am speaking of Dante Alighieri, the author of the *Divine Comedy*; Geoffrey Chaucer, author of *The Canterbury Tales;*

and Erasmus of Rotterdam, author of *In Praise of Folly*. Each of those texts is a masterpiece, and each contains a world of insight and inspiration. And each also clearly lays out the stupidity and moral decrepitude of far too many of the clergy. Think, for instance, of Dante's assignment of numerous priests, bishops, cardinals, and popes to some of the lower circles of hell, or of Chaucer's wicked skewering of clerics in "The Pardoner's Tale," or of Erasmus' mocking of priestly self-importance and duplicity. All three of these authors, it is important to remember, were devout churchmen; but all three were, at the same time, more than willing to complain when ecclesial leaders failed to live up to their calling.

There was a pope in the early sixteenth century who was so morally dysfunctional that his name has become a code word for institutional corruption. I am referring to Rodrigo Borgia, who became Alexander VI upon his election to the papacy. In the course of his clerical career, when he was formally bound to a vow of celibacy, he had a

49

string of mistresses with whom he fathered at least ten illegitimate children, including two who were born during his papacy. Throughout his years of activity within the Church, he was notorious for the two characteristic clerical offenses of simony (buying ecclesial offices) and nepotism (unfairly favoring his family). Like other popes of the Renaissance period, Alexander was also a ruthless military figure, waging war throughout Italy. His death in 1503 was, fittingly enough, prompted by the ingestion of poisoned wine. Alexander's third successor was the son of the great Florentine humanist Lorenzo de' Medici, and upon his election, he took the name Leo X. A sensuous libertine, Leo loved fine food, choice wine, banquets, revelry, and especially the hunt. Even as the Church was facing the crisis of the Protestant Reformation, Leo remained caught up in distractions and trivial amusements. He is reported to have said, soon after his election, "Since God has seen fit to give us the papacy, let us enjoy it."

There is obviously much more that could be recounted under this heading of ecclesiastical corruption, but I would like to focus particular attention on only one more case, since it has so many resonances with our present predicament. In that notorious eleventh century, when the papacy was so compromised, sexual abuse of young people by the clergy was also rampant. The man who, above all others, shed light on this situation and raised his voice in strenuous protest was St. Peter Damian. In the year 1049, Peter, who was at the time prior of a hermitage in Umbria, composed a letter to Pope Leo IX in which he complained of a distinctively foul corruption within the clergy. Not one to mince words, he got specific: "The befouling cancer of sodomy is, in fact, spreading so through the clergy, or rather like a savage beast, is raging with such shameless abandon through the flock of Christ."

By the term "sodomy," Peter Damian meant a range of homosexual behaviors, but what particularly vexed him were acts of sexual predation by older

51

clergy of young boys and the lax attitude of those religious superiors who knew about such outrages yet did nothing to stop them. Some offending priests, he said, even chose sympathetic confessors who would underplay the sin and give only light penances. For them he had choice words: "Listen, you do-nothing superiors of clerics and priests. Listen, and even though you feel sure of yourselves, tremble at the thought that you are partners in the guilt of others, those I mean who wink at the sins of their subjects that need correction and who by ill-considered silence allow them license to sin." But his greatest scorn—and how startlingly contemporary this sounds—was directed to bishops who acted out sexually with young priests and seminarians: "What a vile deed, deserving a flood of bitter tears! If they who approve of these evildoers deserve to die, what condign punishment can be imagined for those who commit these absolutely damnable acts with their spiritual sons?" Relying upon the master metaphor of spiritual fatherhood, St. Peter Damian concluded that all of this abuse

We Have Been Here Before

amounted to a kind of "spiritual incest"—the fathers, as it were, preying sexually on their own children. As I read this *cri de cœur* from a thousand years ago, I can sense the same righteous anger, the same spiritual frustration, the same existential sadness that I sense in so many Catholics today.

Now, not one bit of this historical survey is meant as an excuse, much less a justification, for the wickedness on display in the Church today. But it is indeed meant to place in a wider context what we might be tempted to see as uniquely horrific. We have been here before, and we've survived. I will say more about this in the closing chapter, but a time of crisis is not the moment to abandon the Church; it is the moment to stay and fight— precisely in the spirit of St. Peter Damian.

CHAPTER FOUR

Why Should We Stay?

*I*n the sixth chapter of John's Gospel, there is a scene of absolutely pivotal importance. Finding the Lord's words concerning the Eucharist simply too much to take, the majority of Jesus' followers abandoned him: "Because of this many of his disciples turned back and no longer went about with him." Turning to his inner circle, the tiny band of his most ardent apostles, Jesus said, simply and plaintively, "Do you also wish to go away?" The entire future of the Christian movement was hanging in the balance as Jesus awaited an answer. Finally, Peter spoke: "Lord, to whom can we go? You have the words of eternal life" (John 6:66-68). Now, to be sure, the context today is different, but the fundamental principle remains the same: if you have found in Jesus everlasting life, salvation, the answer to the deepest longing of your heart, then no matter how difficult things become, and no matter how many of your fellows might drift away, you must stay.

As we saw, Paul spoke of the treasure in earthen vessels. I don't think anyone who has read to this point could doubt that I have taken fully into consideration just how fragile and compromised the vessels are and have been. If we look around at the situation today, we see it; if we look back to the Scriptures, it is evident; if we survey the twenty centuries of Church history, we cannot miss it. Yet the treasure remains. And we stay because of the treasure.

In the fourth century, St. Augustine did battle with the Donatists. These were Christians who claimed that priests and bishops who had deserted the Church during times of persecution, and subsequently returned, were not worthy to administer the sacraments. Sensing that the integrity of the Church itself was in question, Augustine raised his voice in eloquent protest, arguing that the sacraments remained valid despite the unworthiness of those at whose hands they were offered. This great teacher of the Church did not deny for a moment the seriousness of the moral offense in question, but he insisted that, despite the sin of the ministers, the grace that they mediate remains.

In the course of this brief chapter, I would like to present the treasure, which is the life of Christ available in and through the Church. This will, quite obviously, not be a detailed theological treatise, but rather a hymn, a poem, a celebration. We do indeed have to look hard at the wickedness in the Church today; but we also have to be clear-eyed about the beauty and veracity and holiness on offer in that same Church. The vessels are all fragile and many of them are downright broken; but we don't stay because of the vessels. We stay because of the treasure.

Before getting to the substance of this chapter, let me make one more rather blunt remark: there is simply never a good reason to leave the Church. Never. Good reasons to criticize Church people?

Plenty. Legitimate reasons to be angry with corruption, stupidity, careerism, cruelty, greed, and sexual misconduct on the part of leaders of the Church? You bet. But grounds for turning away from the grace of Christ in which eternal life is found? No. Never, under any circumstances.

The first dimension of the treasure I would like to present is this: the Church speaks of God. It should come as a surprise to no one that we live in a time, at least in the West, when secularism is dramatically on the rise. For the first time in recorded cultural history, large swaths of the population are explicitly or implicitly denying the existence of God and pretending that fulfillment can be had through the goods and experiences of this world. As recently as fifty years ago, practically nobody, even in Western countries, would have believed this, but now armies of people, especially the young, take it for granted. And this indifference is doing irreparable damage, for—as St. Augustine reminded us long ago—our hearts are wired for God and therefore will remain restless until they rest in God. The best proof of this is that nothing in this world—no amount of money, sex, pleasure, power, or esteem—perfectly quiets the longing of the soul. And as C.S. Lewis insisted, we know this truth most painfully precisely at the *best* moments of life, when we have realized our fondest worldly dreams and yet remain dissatisfied. St. John of the Cross compared the unconditioned desire of the heart to infinitely deep caverns. No amount of finite goods hurled into those abysses will ever fill them up. It is, as the Psalmist sang, only in the infinite God that our souls find rest.

Certainly, one of the reasons for the chronic depression that seems to bedevil so many people today is this loss of a transcendent point of reference. The philosopher Charles Taylor speaks of the "buffered self"—which is to say, the self that is hemmed in, divorced from any contact with what goes beyond this world. Living in that cramped space is simply deadly for the human soul. It is akin to forcing an eagle to occupy a tiny cage. The Church, despite its many failings, speaks of God, of the transcendent

Mystery, of that which corresponds to the most ardent desire of the heart, of the Ultimate Reality—and this word, especially today, is like water in the desert. To Catholic parents, legitimately worried about their sons and daughters compelled to soak in the acids of secularism and materialism, I say, "Don't abandon the Church, which is one of the few remaining institutions in our society that will speak to your children of God!" In both the high and the popular culture, secularist ideology increasingly holds sway, and in the universities, an aggressive atheism is typically the default position. Stay with the Church, because at its best it properly orients the hungry heart.

A second aspect of the treasure: the Church is the Mystical Body of Jesus Christ. According to the ancient faith, Jesus is not one more prophet among many, not simply a spokesperson for God; rather, he is "God from God, light from light, true God from true God." In him, two natures, divine and human, come together. Though this latter formula can sound rather abstract, it is conveying a

fundamental and existentially compelling truth—
namely, that in Jesus, divinity and humanity meet.
In other words, what the heart aches for—real
union with God—is realized, personally and completely, in him. What Israel of the Old Testament
gestured toward through the holy temple, through
the preaching of the prophets, through law and
covenant—real reconciliation with God—is, in
Jesus, an established fact. He is the faithful God
finally and utterly meeting faithful Israel, and hence
he is the savior of the human race. That English
word "savior" is derived from the Latin term *salus*,
meaning health. Through Jesus' perfect humanity,
God "salves" or heals a broken humanity—and
how wonderfully this is exemplified in Jesus' mighty
acts of restoring sight to the blind, hearing to the
deaf, mobility to the crippled, and life to the dead.

And Jesus teaches not simply as one wise person
among many, but as the divine Truth manifesting
itself in human words and in a human voice. Hence,
upon hearing him, the clouding of our minds,
which is itself an effect of sin, is overcome; our

habits, instincts, and manner of seeing, which flow from selfishness, are transformed. In his inaugural address in the Gospel of Mark, Jesus says, simply enough, *metanoiete*, which is usually rendered as "repent" (Mark 1:15). But the word literally means "go beyond the mind you have." And St. Paul urges the earliest Christians, "Let the same mind be in you that was in Christ Jesus" (Phil. 2:5). Like sheep that respond eagerly to the voice of the shepherd, so men and women, up and down the ages, have responded to the voice of Jesus the preacher. In many iconic representations of the Last Supper, St. John, the beloved disciple, is pictured leaning on the breast of Jesus in such a way that his head is aligned just below the Master's head. The point is that he sees the world from the same angle as the Lord; he has the mind of Christ, for he has spent so many years listening to Jesus.

At the climax of his life, Jesus died on a Roman cross, an exquisitely designed instrument of torture. What brought him to such an end? We have to understand that Jesus is consistently presented in the Gospels as a warrior and a king. From the first moments of his life, he is opposed, for we hear that Herod tries to wipe him out and all of Jerusalem trembles in fear of him. From the beginning of his public ministry, his enemies come out to meet him: the demons who scream their recognition of him; the scribes and Pharisees—the official keepers of the religious establishment—who conspire to humiliate him and then to kill him; the ordinary people who call him mad, a drunkard, a trouble-maker. But he fights—not with the weapons of the world or by employing the strategies of worldly rulers, but rather with compassion, forgiveness, nonviolence, the characteristic moves and attitudes of what he calls "the kingdom of God," God's way of ordering things.

As was inevitable, the struggle between the kingdom of God and what John's Gospel calls "the world" came to a climax. Just a week before his death, Jesus entered Jerusalem in the manner of a king, as the prophet Zechariah had said he would, and he was hailed by adoring crowds. But when he caused a ruckus in the temple, calling down judgment upon the holiest place in Israel, he stirred the ferocious opposition of both the Jewish and Roman establishments, the former accusing him of blasphemy and the latter of sedition. On the way to his death, he was met by stupidity, institutional injustice, hatred, cruelty, betrayal, denial, scapegoating, and shocking violence— by all of the darkness of the fallen world. Hanging from the cross, in literally excruciating (*ex cruce*, from the cross) pain, abandoned by his friends, at the limit of physical and psychological agony, he cried out, "My God, my God, why have you abandoned me?" (Matt. 27:46). The still dizzying claim of Christianity is that we are meant to see in that figure not only an unjustly accused man, not simply a heroic martyr, but God himself, having gone to the limits of godforsakenness. And in that heart of darkness, he uttered the prayer, "Father, forgive them, they know not what they do" (Luke 23:34). What this signaled was the swallowing up of all of the world's negativity in the ever-greater divine mercy, the breaking of the power of sin.

But what gives us the confidence to say that this story is more than a hero's tale with a tragic ending? It was what happened on the third day following the terrible execution. Coming to the tomb early on Sunday morning, a number of his disciples found the body of their Lord missing. While they were still wondering what this absence meant, they saw him. Not a ghost, not a fantasy, but *him*. The same Jesus whom they knew, with whom they had eaten and drunk, who had beguiled them with his preaching and healed them of their illnesses, who had walked the roads of Galilee and Judea with them—that Jesus was alive, presenting himself to them. Many people of that time, formed in the Greek philosophical tradition, might have believed in the immortality of the soul, but the first Christians were not talking about Jesus' soul having gone to heaven. Many Jews of that time believed that the dead would be physically raised at the end of time, but the first Christians weren't talking about a general resurrection at the close of the age. They

were describing the bodily resurrection and glori-
fication, in time, of their friend and Lord. And this
meant, in a word, that everything had changed. The
old world was broken, because now they knew that
God's love is more powerful than hatred, cruelty,
injustice, and violence. Even more wonderfully and
unnervingly, they realized that death itself was
overcome. That which had always hung as a dark
cloud over the whole of human life, that which had
haunted the human race from the beginning, that
which had been used by every tyrant in history to
intimidate and manipulate his subjects, was now a
defeated enemy.

And this explains their strange relationship
to the cross of Jesus. A Roman cross was meant
to terrify people into submission. Run afoul of us,
the Roman political leadership said, and we will
hang you, naked, on a device that will guarantee
a slow, painful, and deeply humiliating death. It is
no accident whatsoever that the authorities would
place crosses in very public locations, for they were
meant to be seen. If anything symbolized the terror,

cruelty, and violence of the corrupt world, it was this awful thing. But the first Christians, in a manner that must have struck their listeners as bordering on insanity, held up the cross, spoke of it, celebrated it. Who can forget St. Paul's strange claim: "I decided to know nothing among you except Jesus Christ, and him crucified" (1 Cor. 2:2). This would be roughly akin to someone today announcing that the single theme of his proclamation would be a criminal executed by lethal injection. They could do this only because they were utterly convinced that the Resurrection had disempowered the cross and all that it entailed and the twisted world that made it possible. If I dare to put it this way, they held it up as a kind of taunt: "You think this frightens us? God is more powerful!"

Much of this was summed up in a phrase that was frequently on the lips and under the pen of St. Paul: "Jesus Christ is Lord" (Phil. 2:11). In the culture of that time and place, Caesar was considered the Lord—which is to say, the one to whom final allegiance was due. But the first followers of the risen Jesus knew that the Resurrection had undermined the supremacy of Caesar and all his colleagues and imitators up and down the ages. Now the one to whom ultimate allegiance is due is Jesus, whom Caesar killed but whom God raised up. No wonder that, in Matthew's telling, the death of Jesus was accompanied by an earthquake, for indeed, the cross of Christ represented the shaking of the old order. And what delicious irony in John's telling that Pontius Pilate, Caesar's local representative in Palestine, could put over the cross of the Lord what was meant to be a bit of mockery but what was, in fact, a frank declaration: "Jesus of Nazareth, the King of the Jews" (John 19:19).

I mentioned just a few paragraphs above that the Church is called the Mystical Body of Christ. This characterization implies that the Church is not the "Jesus Christ Society," a gathering of like-minded people who fondly remember the life and works of a distant historical figure, like the International Churchill Society. It is an organism, not an organization. Those who have been grafted on to Jesus Christ are the eyes, ears, hands, feet, and heart through which Jesus continues his properly subversive and re-creative work in the world.

And this brings us to a third aspect of the treasure: the Holy Spirit. The first followers of the risen Christ felt that they had been inhabited by the Spirit of their Lord, which lifted them up, gave them courage, breathed through their words and actions. In the Acts of the Apostles, we hear that the Spirit was sent to the Church by the ascended Jesus. We must never think of the Ascension as Jesus' leave-taking, but rather his assuming, in the manner of a general commanding a field of battle, a vantage point from which he directs the operations of his Church. It is this same Holy Spirit who, throughout the history of the Church to the present moment, gives vitality and energy to the Mystical Body.

And now that we've spoken of the Holy Spirit, we are ready to present a fourth dimension of the treasure: the strange doctrine of the Trinity, which presents the one God as a unity of three persons.

I realize that this sort of language can seem either hopelessly abstract or just incoherent, but it actually speaks a truth that is of central and saving significance. The Father sent his only Son into the world, all the way to the limits of godforsakenness, and then, in the Holy Spirit, he drew the Son back to himself. But on that return journey, the Son carried with him, at least in principle, all those he had reached through his descent. We are saved precisely because God opened himself up in a great act of love, the Father and the Son gathering us into the Holy Spirit. This outward manifestation of God's love reflects, the Church teaches, an even more primordial set of relationships within God's own inner life. From all eternity, the Father speaks the Son, who is a perfect image of the Father; the Son and the Father look at one another and they fall in love. The love that they breathe back and forth is the *Spiritus Sanctus*, literally "the holy breath." Therefore, as G.K. Chesterton observed, the Trinitarian doctrine is simply a technically precise way of saying that God *is* love. In his very unity, there is a play between lover (the Father), beloved (the Son), and the love they share (the Holy Spirit). Almost every religion and religious philosophy would defend the proposition that God loves or that love is one of God's attributes; but only Christianity makes the odd claim that love is what God *is*. The Church bears this truth to the world: what is ultimately real is love. I cannot imagine a more indispensable message, especially now.

The Christ-life that we have been describing comes into us, the Church teaches, through the sacraments, and this brings me to a fifth feature of the treasure. Baptism, Confirmation, and the Eucharist initiate us into the life; Marriage and Holy Orders give that life missionary direction; Confession and the Anointing of the Sick restore the life when it has been lost. As necessary as food and drink are to the body, so are the sacraments for the health of the soul. Now, Thomas Aquinas said that, though all the sacraments contain the power of Jesus, only the Eucharist contains Jesus himself. When we consume the Eucharist, we are taking the whole Christ—body, blood, soul, and divinity—into ourselves, becoming thereby conformed to him in the most literal sense. Through this great sacrament, we are Christified, eternalized, deified, made ready for life on high with God. And as we saw earlier, St. Augustine clarified that the validity of the Eucharist is in no way compromised by the immorality of the priest involved in its consecration. Therefore, let me state it bluntly: the Eucharist is the single most important reason for staying faithful to the Church. You can't find it anywhere else; and no wickedness on the part of priests or bishops can affect it.

Those who have put on Jesus Christ, who have been divinized through the sacraments, who have the Holy Spirit in them, who have become conformed radically to the Trinitarian love are called saints. The entire purpose of the Church is to produce them, and they are a sixth dimension of the treasure. Even as we look around and see sickening corruption in the Church today, and even as we look back at myriad examples of immorality on the part of ecclesial leaders, we must never overlook the saints, who are present in every age and are operative in the world now. They are the lights shining in the gloom.

We remember St. Paul, who careered around the world to announce the kingship of Jesus and who wrote of his Lord in words of surpassing eloquence; we think of Sts. Polycarp, Sebastian, Felicity, Perpetua, Lucy, and Agnes, all of whom witnessed to Christ with their lives; we recall St. Francis, the troubadour of Lady Poverty, who revolutionized medieval Europe by his reckless abandon to God's providence; we ruminate on St. Catherine of Siena, who looked with mystical vision into heaven and tended the wounds of the poorest here on earth; we celebrate St. Francis Xavier, who crossed oceans to proclaim the Gospel to those who had never heard of Christ; we think of St. Francis de Sales, who showed how the most ordinary things of life can be sanctified; we reverence St. Peter Claver, whose service to African captives coming to the New World was so devoted that he was called "the slave of the slaves"; we hold up St. Damien of Molokai, who volunteered to care for lepers in Hawaii, knowing that he would never leave their island enclave alive; we consider St. Teresa of Kolkata, who quit her ministry at a relatively prosperous school and walked into the worst slum in the world in order to help the poorest of the poor; and we remember Pope St. John Paul II, who as a young man survived the outrages of both Nazism and Communism and who, as pope, brought down a wicked political system—not by leading armies but by unleashing the power of the Gospel.

Among the saints we find the brilliant Thomas Aquinas and the scholastically challenged Jean Vianney; the wealthy Thomas More and the abjectly poor Benedict Joseph Labre; the warrior Joan of Arc and the pacifists Nereus and Achilleus; the mystic John of the Cross and the social activist Oscar Romero; King Louis IX and the humble porter André Bessette; John Henry Newman, who lived to be ninety, and Dominic Savio, who died as a boy; Thérèse of Lisieux, who spent her entire religious life in a tiny convent in an obscure town, and Frances Xavier Cabrini, who crossed oceans and continents; Ignatius of Loyola, who walked only with difficulty, and Pier Giorgio Frassati, who loved to climb mountains. The point is that each of the saints, in his or her own utterly unique manner, shows forth some aspect of God's beauty and perfection. No one saint could ever exhaustively express the infinite holiness of God; and therefore, God makes saints the way he makes plants and animals and stars: exuberantly, effervescently, and with a preference for wild diversity. The one thing, of course, that all the saints have in common is that they are friends of Christ, and this is why we, who are striving to deepen our own friendship with the Lord, find such powerful fellowship with them. Though we are separated from the saints by culture, personality, and in some cases, oceans of time, we are joined to them because we share a best friend. This is a crucial reason why we stay connected to the Church. Though there are, God knows, lots and lots of people, even among the top leadership of the Church, who fall far short of holiness, the saints remain as beacons, models, companions on the way.

Just a week or so before I composed these words, a national poll showed that, in the wake of the scandals, 37% of Catholics are seriously considering leaving the Church. I understand the frustration and the rage that lie behind this consideration. But I also hope that this particular chapter has made clear that I don't think such a move is warranted. In the end, we are not Catholics because our leaders are flawless, but because we find the claims of Catholicism both compelling and beautiful. We are Catholics because the Church speaks of the Trinitarian God whose very nature is love; of Jesus the Lord, crucified and risen from the dead; of the Holy Spirit, who inspires the followers of Christ up and down the ages; of the sacraments, which convey the Christ-life to us; and of the saints, who are our friends in the spiritual order. This is the treasure; this is why we stay.

CHAPTER FIVE

The Way Forward

*T*he devil, with the cooperation of lots of people inside the leadership of the Church, has produced a masterpiece, and many, many Catholics are naturally angry and even tempted to give up on the operation. The Catholic Church, it seems, is just too corrupt, too compromised, too wicked and clueless. Yet the Sacred Scriptures shed considerable light on the dynamics that produced this very problem; the history of the Church reveals that we have found ourselves, in point of fact, in worse situations and have survived; and the all too human vessels in which the grace of Christ is found don't finally obviate that grace. If you can accept all of this, you are willing to consider a way forward. Though you might still feel a temptation to leave, you are persuaded that the better option is to stay and fight, especially on behalf of the victims. In this final section, I would like to explore this properly pugnacious path.

A first step, necessary but inadequate, is to make serious institutional reforms. And I want to speak clearly and positively here about what the Church has already done in this regard. After the first great outbreak of this tragedy in 2002, the bishops of the United States gathered for their annual spring assembly in Dallas. In the course of that crucially important meeting, they hammered out a series of protocols to govern the handling of sexual abuse by Catholic clergy. A simple internet search will provide the Charter for the Protection of Children and Young People in full detail, but I want to highlight just a few features for our purposes. First, the bishops agreed to a zero-tolerance policy regarding the sexual abuse of minors. For decades, Church leadership had seen such behavior as simply a sin that could be dealt with through prayer, spiritual counseling, and perhaps an extended retreat. Then, appreciating the unreliability of this approach, they adopted a psychodynamic framework of interpretation and concluded that therapy and other forms of psychological therapy would deal with the problem. To be fair, many bishops in the seventies and eighties reassigned offending priests after they had received assurance from psychological counselors that these men were fit for ministry. Within the context of understanding in vogue at the time, these decisions seemed defensible. But the whirlwind and maelstrom of 2002 disclosed that no amount of such therapy could definitively "solve" the problem of sexual abuse. And therefore, "one strike and you're out" became, after Dallas, the policy. Relatedly, any charge of sexual abuse of a minor that comes to the Church's attention must be reported, without delay, to the relevant civil authorities.

A second key feature of the Dallas accords is the insistence upon background checks, not only for priests but for any employee of the Catholic Church. Anyone with an incident of sexual abuse on his or her record simply cannot minister in any capacity within the structure of the Church. When I was rector of Mundelein Seminary in the Archdiocese of Chicago, I had the obligation to preside over the admission process for all prospective students. I can testify that criminal background checks, careful psychological screening, and numerous interviews were *de rigueur* for every candidate. When I became Auxiliary Bishop of Los Angeles, I willingly submitted, within a few days of my arrival in LA, to fingerprinting and an updated background check.

A third element of the Dallas protocols is specialized training—again, for any and all people who work for or minister within the Church—in recognizing the signs of sexual abuse and in the procedure for reporting the offense to the police.

A fourth requirement is one to which I would like to draw particular attention. Any accusation against a priest that is deemed credible results in the immediate removal of that priest from ministry and the engagement of a lay review board, which has the responsibility of investigating the case and making a recommendation to the relevant bishop or archbishop. This involvement of lay people— competent in law, psychology, criminal investigation, etc.—assures that clergy are not judged simply by other clergy, who would perhaps be prejudiced in favor of their brothers.

Finally, the compliance of each diocese or archdiocese with these norms is guaranteed by the oversight of a National Review Board—again, largely composed of lay people—who perform regular audits.

There is more that I could say about the Dallas protocols, but these are the principal features. And the plain truth is this: these institutional changes *have* made a substantial difference. Numerous careful studies have revealed that instances of clergy sex abuse peaked in the 1960s and 1970s, declining steadily thereafter, and precipitously after 2002, so that now the reporting of new cases is down to a trickle. I wouldn't dream of denying or underplaying the horrors reported in the Pennsylvania Attorney General report already cited, but I would say that it is regrettable in the extreme that even churchgoing Catholics tended to believe that the terrible instances mentioned in that study were recent cases. In point of fact, of the four hundred or so crimes reported, precisely two occurred after 2002.

In the wake of the McCarrick outrage, a general cry went up for similar regulations to govern the reporting of abuse on the part of bishops. As I write these words, the bishops of the United States are refining protocols precisely of this nature, instituting largely lay-led regional review boards to receive and investigate accusations against bishops. Once again, these institutional changes aren't going to solve the problem definitively, but they will represent an enormously important step in the right direction. I believe that another essential move, if the Church is serious about preventing McCarrick-like situations going forward, is to launch a formal investigation, both on this side of the Atlantic and in Rome, to determine how someone like Theodore McCarrick, whose serious misbehavior was well known, could possibly have risen so high in the government of the Church.

But much more is needed than a tightening of protocols, as crucial as that is. What is especially needed is a deep and abiding spiritual reform. And this ought to begin with the priesthood. Can anyone doubt at this point that there has been a serious rot in the Catholic priesthood? Mind you, I'm not blaming all of my brothers; I'm not saying all priests are equally guilty; I'm not denying that there are real saints and heroes in the ranks of the priesthood. However, the scandals of the last many decades—both the crimes themselves and the cover-ups—disclose that something has gone deeply wrong. That significant numbers of priests felt insufficient moral restraint when it came to physically, psychologically, and spiritually abusing some of the most vulnerable members of their flocks is simply unconscionable. And that a not inconsiderable number of bishops felt that it was permissible to shuffle offending priests from parish to parish, without even a word of warning to the people, clearly putting children in acute danger, beggars belief. Something in the moral compass of these men was haywire. Attempts to explain the crisis by noting that the percentage of abusers among priests is roughly equivalent to the national average don't satisfy. Have we settled for a bar that low? When it comes to moral and spiritual integrity, priests are meant to be leaders, exemplars. Hewing to the national average of sex abuse is hardly anything to crow about.

Moreover, we have to look beyond the explicit offenders and raise some serious questions about the clerical culture that made this kind of abuse and its cover-up possible. A moral relativism, especially in regard to matters sexual, came to be taken for granted in the years following the Second Vatican Council, and this attitude was adopted by too many within the priesthood itself. How many priests and bishops saw what was happening but looked the other way, convinced that it was not their business to question the moral decision of a brother? Or how many priests and bishops simply lacked the courage to engage in fraternal correction, especially if that meant losing a friend? Or how many went even further, overlooking or condoning these aberrant sexual expressions because "Father has given up so much"? Or how many priests and bishops acted like David, striding on the roof of his palace and ordering that Bathsheba come to them? Priests had (and have) a good deal of power over their people, and this power can be used for enormous good and for enormous wickedness. What should have been a liberating and life-giving authority became manipulative in the extreme. And how many bishops and diocesan officials winked at sexual crimes, persuaded that the Church had moved beyond an obsession with sex?

Therefore, a renewal of the priesthood is imperative. I don't think for a moment that a change in its essential structure or discipline is called for. In my judgment, it is naïve in the extreme to imagine that allowing priests to marry or women to be priests will greatly ameliorate this situation. The last time I checked, all human beings are fallen, and celibate males do not have a monopoly on selfishness, stupidity, and wickedness. Rather, what is needed is a reinvigoration of the priesthood, a rededication to its ideals. As Fulton Sheen said, the priest is not his own, for he belongs to Jesus Christ. He acts in the very person of the Lord, speaking his words and drawing people into his power. Accordingly, a priest must be devoted to Christ, conformed to him at all levels of his being. His mind, his will, his passions, his body, his private life, his public life, and his friendships must all belong to the Lord. Period. A priest whose central preoccupation is money or pleasure or power or career advancement or fame will, sooner or later, fall apart and wreak havoc around him. The institutional reputation of the Church must never become the supreme value for any Church representative. The institution serves the people of God, and if any one of the people of God is in danger, action must be taken, even if this means that the institution will suffer embarrassment or financial loss.

And the needed renewal must be broader still, very much including lay men and women. In saying this, I am by no means trying to exculpate priests or to imply that everyone is equally to blame. But priests do not arise from a vacuum. They come, in the overwhelming majority of cases, from Catholic families, and they are (or at least ought to be) shaped by a Catholic culture. Therefore, fellow Catholics, this scandal is *our* problem. All of us Catholics ought to appreciate this painful time, therefore, as an invitation to rediscover and to deepen our own baptismal identity as priests, prophets, and kings. Priests are those who are committed, all the way down, to holiness of life; prophets are those who have dedicated themselves to proclaiming Christ to everybody; and kings are those who are resolved to order the world, as far as they can, to God's purposes. What does it say about the priestly resolve of the baptized in this country that 75% of us regularly stay away from Mass, that prayer which Vatican II described as "the source and summit of the Christian life"? Or that the numbers of those seeking Baptism, Marriage, and Confirmation in the Church are trending dramatically downwards? And what does it say about our prophetic effectiveness that young people are abandoning our Church in droves? Obviously, the full exploration of this complex phenomenon would require another entire book, but suffice it to say that we (and I do mean *we*) have been, rather obviously, derelict in our obligation to proclaim Christ and to make membership in his Church appealing to a culture grown skeptical and secularist. And what does it say about our effectiveness as kings when our society seems, more and more, to run on purely materialist and egotistic principles, and when poll after poll reveals that, on the major moral issues under discussion today, Catholics more or less track with the secularist consensus?

The bottom line is this: if we want holier priests, we all have to become holier ourselves. Cardinal Francis George once characterized clericalism as an attitude predicated upon the assumption that the link between Holy Orders and Baptism has been severed. He was implying that priesthood, authentically interpreted, is in service of the baptized and not the prerogative of a privileged class. But there is another way to understand his intuition—namely, that the baptized are the community from which priests come and from which they ought to receive ongoing sustenance. A better and stronger laity shapes a better and stronger (and less clericalist) priesthood.

As the ancient Roman cultural order was collapsing in the sixth century, a young man called Benedict, as we saw, elected to absent himself from the city of Rome where he had been studying and to take up residence in a cave in the wilderness. There he lived for three years, communing with God and seeking perfection of life. In time, others came to join him, and from this original band there grew the Benedictine Order. In the course of centuries, the Benedictines effectively re-civilized Europe, preserving what was best from the ancient world and providing a framework, both economic and spiritual, for the development of communities and cities. In a moment of crisis both moral and cultural, God inspired this man to lead a movement of renewal.

In the late twelfth and early thirteenth centuries, the European clergy was marked by corruption, laxity, and worldliness. Far too many bishops and priests were not living in accord with their priestly promises, and far too many of the Benedictine houses that once had brought the Gospel and civic order to the community were now simply centers of commerce and political power. From the little town of Assisi in Umbria there came a simple man named Francesco, who endeavored to live the Gospel in its most radical form, embracing poverty, the lifestyle of an itinerant preacher, and radical trust in God's providence. To this odd troubadour of Christ came dozens, then hundreds, then thousands of people, eager to share his life. The Franciscan movement,

94

within a few decades, had established itself as a reforming force all over the Christian West. On clear display was the familiar pattern of crisis and renovation.

In the wake of the Protestant Reformation in the sixteenth century, when Western Christianity found itself bitterly divided and many were abandoning the classical Catholic faith, a young man called Íñigo de Loyola, like his spiritual forebear Benedict, felt called to spend a considerable time in a cave, purging himself of attachments and learning to follow the promptings of the Holy Spirit. On the basis of that experience, Ignatius (he had Latinized his name) composed a series of "exercises" designed to help people discern the will of God in their lives. Some who practiced these exercises formed a family around Ignatius, and from that family grew the Jesuit order, which spread with extraordinary rapidity throughout the Catholic world and which gave rise to an army of poets, missionaries, evangelists, and theologians, who addressed the spiritual crisis of that moment.

After the French Revolution, when Europe was in political turmoil and the faith under assault from rationalizing and secularizing ideologies, a whole coterie of orders and movements arose: the Oblates of Mary Immaculate, the Congregation of Holy Cross, the Society of Mary, and many others. Their purpose was to preach, teach, and evangelize those who had effectively forgotten their Catholicism. So fruitful were these communities that many of them sent missionaries to the far ends of the world. Once again, suffering and corruption called forth a response of the Spirit.

Many more tales with this theme could be told, but the point is this: we find ourselves at one of these decisive moments. Who can deny that a deep and abiding corruption has invaded the Mystical Body of Christ? Who is so blind not to see that the pressing need of our time is a purification of the Church? And therefore, who can fail to appreciate that this is precisely the time for new orders, new movements, new works of the Spirit! Whereas the reforms that I have enumerated so far were largely clerical, I believe that our time calls for renewal movements that will involve both priests and laity. Perhaps Communion and Liberation, the Alliance for Catholic Education (ACE) movement, Opus Dei, L'Arche, Cursillo, and the Fellowship of Catholic University Students (FOCUS) give some indication of what forms these could take. But something new must come forth, something specifically fitted to our time and designed to respond to the particular corruption that currently besets us. Above all, we need saints, marked by holiness of course, but also by intelligence, an understanding of the culture, and the willingness to try something fresh. Somewhere in the Church right now is a new Benedict, a new Francis, a new Ignatius, a new Teresa of Kolkata, a new Dorothy Day. This is your time!

I know many Catholics are sorely tempted just to give up on the Church, to join another religious group, or perhaps to become one of the religiously unaffiliated. But this is not the time to leave; it is the time to stay and fight. If I may, I'd like to make one more historical reference, this one to a key moment in our political history. By the 1850s, it had become unmistakably clear to Abraham Lincoln that slavery was not only a moral outrage but also an institution that posed a mortal threat to American democracy. One can hear his arguments along these lines in the great speeches he gave while debating Stephen Douglas during the 1858 Illinois senatorial campaign. But nowhere was his case more pithily put than in his famous address before the Illinois General Assembly just after his nomination for the Senate. "A house divided against itself cannot stand. I believe that this government cannot endure permanently half-slave and half-free."

It was this conviction that led Lincoln, upon becoming President in 1861, to accept and prosecute a terrible war. Midway through that conflict, while dedicating a cemetery for those who died in its decisive battle, Lincoln explained why he continued to fight: "Four score and seven years ago our fathers brought forth, on this continent, a new nation, conceived in liberty, and dedicated to the proposition that all men are created equal. Now we are engaged in a great civil war, testing whether that nation, or any nation so conceived, and so dedicated, can long endure." There were indeed many people in the North who, appalled at the losses on the battlefield and less than persuaded of the utility of the war, were rancorously calling for Lincoln to give up, to let the Confederacy have what it wanted. But the President knew that something more than military victory or national pride was at stake in the struggle; he knew that slavery constituted a rot upon American democracy, a disease that undermined the principles of our founders. Therefore, despite the pain, he had to fight.

I understand that it's not a perfect analogy, but I think it sheds at least some light on the present situation in the Church. The sexual abuse of young people by some priests and the countenancing of that abuse by some bishops is more than a moral problem; it is a rot, a disease, a threat to the great principles of the Church that we hold dear. Yes, an easy option is to cut and run, to give up on the operation. But if you believe, as I do, in those doctrines and practices and convictions that I mentioned in the fourth section of this book, if you think it is indispensable that the Mystical Body of Jesus Christ abides as a light to the world, then take the Lincoln option: stay and fight!

Fight by raising your voice in protest; fight by writing a letter of complaint; fight by insisting that protocols be followed; fight by reporting offenders; fight by pursuing the guilty until they are punished; fight by refusing to be mollified by pathetic excuses.

But above all, fight by your very holiness of life; fight by becoming the saint that God wants you to be; fight by encouraging a decent young man to become a priest; fight by doing a Holy Hour every day for the sanctification of the Church; fight by coming to Mass regularly; fight by evangelizing; fight by doing the corporal and spiritual works of mercy.

God is love, and he has won the victory through the cross and resurrection of Jesus. Therefore, we inhabit what is finally a divine comedy, and we know that the followers of Jesus are on the winning side. Perhaps the very best way to be a disciple of Jesus right now is to stay and fight for his Church.

Lord Jesus Christ, through your Incarnation you accepted a human nature and lived a real, human life. Setting aside the glory of your divinity, you met us face to face in the vulnerability of our humanity.

Though without sin, you accepted sinners, offering forgiveness and placing yourself before even the most unworthy as a servant and a friend. You became small and weak in the estimation of the powerful, so that you might elevate to glory the small and weak of the world.

Your descent into our nature was not without risk, as it exposed you to the assaults of the darkest and most terrifying of humanity's fallen desires—our cruelty and narrowness, our deceptions and our denials. All this culminated in the cross, where your divine love was met with the full fury of our malice, our violence, and our estrangement from your grace.

103

*You offered yourself to us with innocence and receptivity,
and this was met with the abuse of your body, humiliation
and mockery, betrayal and isolation, torture and death.
All this—even the dereliction of feeling abandoned by
God—you accepted. You became a victim, so that all those
victimized since the beginning of the world would know you
as their advocate. You went into the darkness, so that all
those compelled into the dark by human wickedness would
discover in you a radiant light.*

*Grant we pray, O Lord, healing for all victims of sexual
abuse. Purify your Church of corruption. Bring justice
to those who have been wronged. Grant consolation to all
who are afflicted. Cast your light to banish the shadows of
deception. Manifest to all your advocacy of those who have
been so cruelly hurt, and your judgment upon those who,
having perpetrated such crimes, remain unrepentant. Compel
those in your Church whom you have entrusted to safeguard
the innocent and act on behalf of the victims to be vigilant
and zealous in their duties. Restore faith to those from
whom it has been stolen, and hope to those who
have despaired.*

Christ the Victim, we call out to you!
Strengthen your faithful to accept the mission placed before
us, a mission of holiness and truth. Inspire us to become
advocates of those who have been harmed. Grant us strength
to fight for justice. Impart to us courage so that we might
forthrightly face the challenges to come. Raise up saints from
your Church, and grant us the grace to become the saints
you desire us to be. This we ask of you, who live and reign
with the Father and the Holy Spirit, one God,
forever and ever.
Amen.

37% of Catholics are considering leaving the Church due to the sexual abuse crisis . . .

This book can help.

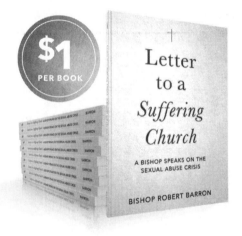

Order more copies of this book for your friends, family, or parish, and access free resources for discussing the sexual abuse crisis, by visiting:

SufferingChurchBook.com